365
Reflections on
SISTERS

365
Reflections on
SISTERS

Selected and arranged by
Dahlia Porter and Gabriel Cervantes

Adams Media Corporation
Holbrook, Massachusetts

Published by Adams Media Corporation
260 Center Street, Holbrook, MA 02343

ISBN: 1-55850-810-4

Printed in Canada.

J I H G F E D C B

Library of Congress Cataloging-in-Publication Data
365 reflections on sister / edited by Dahlia Porter and Gabriel Cervantes.
p.   cm.
Includes bibliographical references.
ISBN 1-55850-810-4 (paperback)
1. Sisters—Quotations, maxims, etc. I. Porter, Dahlia. II. Cervantes, Gabriel.
PN6084.S56A16   1997
306.875—dc21   97-28114
CIP

This book is available at quantity discounts for bulk purchases.
For information, call 1-800-872-5627 (in Massachusetts, 617-767-8100).

Visit our home page at http://www.adamsmedia.com

To Freeda
for we are sisters of the soul

Contents

❧

Sharing

*O*ne's sister is a part of one's essential self, an eternal presence of one's heart and soul and memory.

—*Susan Cahill*

$\mathcal{M}$y sister taught me everything I need to know, and she was only in the sixth grade at the time.

— *Linda Sunshine*

*O*nce, when I was very little, she made me supremely happy by rousing me before four o'clock in the morning, dressing me hurriedly, and taking me out with her for a walk across the graveyard and through the dewy fields. The birds were singing, and the sun was just rising, and we were walking toward the east, hand in hand.

—*Lucy Larcom, of her sister*

*T*here is no time like the old time,
when you and I were young!

—*Oliver Wendell Holmes*

$\mathcal{T}$he desire to be and have a sister
is a primitive and profound one
that may have everything or nothing to
do with the family a woman is born to. It
is a desire to know and be known by
somebody who shares blood and body,
history and dreams, common ground
and the unknown adventures of the
future, darkest secrets and the glassiest
beads of truth.

—*Elizabeth Fishel*

$\mathcal{N}$o one knows better than a
sister how we grew up,
and who our friends, teachers and
favorite toys were. No one knows better
than she . . .

—Dale V. Atkins

$\mathcal{T}$o be my best I need you
swimming beside me.

—*Mariah Burton Nelson*

Sisters—they share the agony and the exhilaration. As youngsters they may share popsicles, chewing gum, hair dryers and bedrooms. When they grow up, they share confidences, careers and children, and some even chat for hours every day.

—*Roxanne Brown*

*T*here came a time in my own life
when it suddenly became clear
to me that my sister was the one person
who had known me for the longest
time. . . . In all the things we have
shared—earache, chickenpox, measles,
sweets, toys, books, love, ambition,
shame, fear, to name a few, our two
voices have been the most consistently
shared. . . .

—*Elizabeth Jolley*

*T*here can never be enough said of the virtues, dangers, the power of a shared laugh.

—*Françoise Sagan*

$\mathcal{N}$ot what we give, but what we
share —
For the gift without the giver is bare.

—*James Russell Lowell*

She shared much with her sister—the absence of a father, the presence of a shadowy unhappy mother. They had one bike and one sled between them, and had learned long ago that these possessions were not worth the fights.

—*Ann McGovern*

There is only one real
deprivation, I
decided this morning, and that is not to
be able to give one's gifts to those one
loves most.

—*May Sarton*

*L*ast night Margot and I were lying side by side in my bed. It was incredibly cramped, but that's what made it fun.

—*Anne Frank,*
of her sister

*I*nstead of being a static one-time event, bonding is a process, a dynamic and continuous one.

—*Julius Segal*

$\mathcal{I}$f you and your sister take time to do things one-on-one, away from the extended family, a new pattern of dealing with each other—and a new friendship—is free to emerge.

—*Kim Wright Wiley*

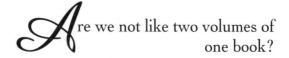

re we not like two volumes of
one book?

—*Marceline Desbordes-Valmore*

[*W*e] started playing together professionally not because we loved the repertory for duo-pianists—we didn't even know it then!—but because we didn't want to separate.

—*Katia Labeque*

$\mathcal{W}$ith the two of them it was just as it is with the honeysuckle that attaches itself to the hazel tree: when it has wound and attached and worked itself around the trunk, the two can survive together; but if someone tries to separate them, the hazel dies quickly and the honeysuckle with it.

—*Marie de France*

*I*f Cassandra were going to have her head cut off, Jane would insist on sharing her fate.

— Cassandra Austen,
of her daughters

$\mathcal{W}$e were friends throughout life, with that intimacy, but also— as children—the squabbling that resulted from sharing a bed for so many years: our parents' discarded double bed, after they had become so modern as to acquire separate English iron beds.

—Alva Myrdal,
of her sister

When we were thirteen our parents got us twin beds. Know what we did? We put a violin case in her bed, covered it up, and the two of us slept in mine. By fifteen, it got doggone crowded in there.

—*Abigail Van Buren,*
of her sister Ann Landers

he three of us shared a bedroom, and the bed was our stage. Sug was the Teacher, Beverly was the Mother, and I was the Student, Daisy. Sug would lie flat on the bed and hold me up in the air with her feet on my stomach, and I would pretend to fly and dance, waving my arms aroundwildly. . . . Eventually we became pretty elaborate in our experiments and my head went through the wall on several occasions.

— *Suzanne Farrell,*
of her sisters, Donna and Beverly

*W*e slept in the same room in the same bed, and she always woke me up when she came in from a date. We'd lie there and whisper and giggle with the dying firelight flickering against the bedroom walls, and I thought she was the neatest thing that ever was. I wanted to be just like her.

—Minnie Pearl,
of her sister

$\mathcal{T}$he sharing of joy, whether physical, emotional, psychic or intellectual, forms a bridge between the sharers which can be the basis for understanding much of what is not shared between them, and lessens the threat of their difference.

—*Audre Lorde*

She took care of me, protected me.

—*Lynn Redgrave,*
of her sister Vanessa

One of the nicest things about those early years on the bus was being together with Louise and Irlene, just as we had been as children. . . . I was still able to play Big Sister to the hilt, coaching my sisters about their roles in the band but also relying on them for help with Matthew.

—Barbara Mandrell

$\mathcal{W}$e just had things together, and
we understood the world.

—*Debra Spark,*
of her sister

*Y*et still my fate permits me this
relief,
To write to lovely Delia all
my grief.
To you alone I venture to complain;
From other hourly strive to hide my
pain.

—Abigail Colman Dennie,
in a letter to her sister

Shared joy is double joy, and shared sorrow is half-sorrow.

Swedish proverb

She has three sisters, Lethean, Evie
    and Ora Gilder:
When they aggravate her she wants to
    pinch
their habits off like potato bugs off the leaf.
But she meets them each weekend for cards
    and jokes
while months go by without her speaking to
    her brother.

—*Minnie Bruce Pratt*

$\mathcal{I}$f sisters were free to express how they really feel, parents would hear this: "Give me all the attention and all the toys and send Rebecca to live with Grandma."

—*Linda Sunshine*

Your sister is the only creature on earth who shares your heritage, history, environment, DNA, bone structure, and contempt for stupid Aunt Gertie.

—*Linda Sunshine*

If your sister is in a tearing hurry to go out and cannot catch your eye, she's wearing your best sweater.

—*Pam Brown*

When someone came to the house they would bring two dolls, one for Grace and one for me.... Years later, when I visited the palace, I looked into her closet and saw all her old dolls. I said, "My God, Grace, you still have those dolls?" And she said, "Don't you still have your dolls?" I said, "No, we destroyed mine playing with them."

—*Lizanne Kelly,*
of her sister Princess Grace

*A*ll who would win joy, must
share it; happiness was
born a twin.

—Lord Byron

According to popular myth, sisters exist on the same side of the closed door, sharing teddy bears and secrets in the privacy of a common bedroom.

—*Marianne Paul*

$\mathcal{M}$y sister had a game . . . called "The Elder Sister." The theme was that in our family was an elder sister, senior to my sister and myself. She was mad and lived in a cave at Corbin's Head, but sometimes she came to the house. . . . Why did I *like* being terrified?

—*Agatha Christie*

*S*ome of the most rewarding and
beautiful moments of a
friendship happen in the unforseen open
spaces between planned activities. It is
important that you allow these
spaces to exist.

—Christine Leefeldt and Ernest Callenbach

A ship is floating in the harbor now,
A wind is hovering o'er the
mountain's brow . . .
The halcyons brood around the
foamless isles;
The treacherous ocean has forsworn
its wiles;
The merry mariners are bold and free:
Say, my sister's heart, wilt thou sail
with me?

—*Percy Bysshe Shelley*

There's a special kind of freedom sisters enjoy. Freedom to share innermost thoughts, to ask a favor, to show their true feelings. The freedom to simply be themselves.

—*Anonymous*

$\mathscr{I}$t is true that I was born in Iowa, but I can't speak for my twin sister.

—*Abigail Van Buren*

*L*oving a sister is an unconditional, narcissistic and complicated devotion that approximates a mother's love. . . . sisters are inescapably connected, shaped by the same two parents, the same trove of memory and experience.

—*Mary Bruno*

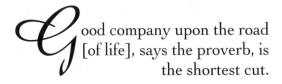

*G*ood company upon the road
[of life], says the proverb, is
the shortest cut.

—Oliver Goldsmith

$\mathcal{W}$e know one another's faults,
virtues, catastrophes,
mortifications, triumphs, rivalries,
desires, and how long we can each hang
by our hands to a bar. We have been
banded together under pack codes and
tribal laws.

—*Rose Macauley*

*P*leasures afford more delight
when shared with others; to
enjoy them in solitude is a dreary thing.

—*Dio Chrysostom*

My sister! ('tis a wish of mine)
Now that our morning meal
is done,
Make haste, your morning take resign;
Come forth and feel the sun.

One moment now may give us more
Than years of toiling reason;
Our minds shall drink at every pore
The spirit of the season.

Then come, my Sister!
Come, I pray,
With speed put on your woodland dress;
And bring no book: for this one day
We'll give to idleness.

— *William Wordsworth,*
"To My Sister"

*O*ften, in old age, they become each other's chosen and most happy companions. In addition to their shared memories of childhood and of their relationship to each other's children, they share memories of the same homemaking style, and the same small prejudices about housekeeping that carry the echoes of their mother's voice.

—*Margaret Mead,*
of her sisters

*S*o closely interwoven have been our lives, our purposes, and experiences that, separated we have a feeling of incompleteness — united, such strength of self-assertion that no ordinary obstacles, differences, or dangers ever appear to us insurmountable.

—*Elizabeth Cady Stanton*

Caring

*I*s solace anywhere
more comforting
than in the arms
of a sister?

—*Alice Walker*

*T*here are the people whom one loves immediately and forever. Even to know they are alive in the world with us is quite enough.

—*Nancy Spain*

*H*allie and I . . . were all that
was. The image in the
mirror that proves you are still here. We
had exactly one sister apiece. We grew
up knowing the simple arithmetic of
scarcity. A sister is more precious than
an eye.

—*Barbara Kingsolver*

$\mathcal{L}$ove is a verb.

—*Clare Booth Luce*

$\mathcal{I}$ was always putting myself in my sister's place, adopting her credulousness, and even her memories, I saw, could be made mine. It was Isobel I imagined as the eternal heroine — never myself. I substituted her feelings for my own, and her face for any face described. Whatever the author's intentions, the heroine was my sister.

—*Mavis Gallant*

[*My* sister] accommodates me, never reproaches me with her doctrine, never tries to change me. She accepts and loves me, despite our differences.

—*Joy Harjo*

When Doren was three years old she informed our parents she had to have a baby sister. A year later I was born. Doren often reminded me I had her to thank for this. Was I supposed to feel grateful, needed, loved? I never quite knew, but I know I believed it was my sister's idea that I come into being. I came into the world, then, Doren's child.

— *Cathy Arden*

*O*ur love for each other has been the torment of our lives hitherto. I am most seriously intending to bend the whole force of my mind to counteract this, and I think I see some prospect of success.

—Mary Anne Lamb,
of her brother Charles

ow selfhood begins with a walking away, and love is proven in the letting go.

—*Cecil Day Lewis*

$\mathcal{M}$y Sister! With a thrilling word
Let thoughts unnumbered wildly spring!
What echoes in my heart are stirred,
While thus I touch the trembling string.

—*Margaret Davidson*

The true way of softening one's troubles is to solace those of others.

—*Madame de Maintenon*

My friend; my brother! you are the last cord that binds me to the world.

—*Jane Porter*

*B*ut oh! If grief thy steps
attend,
If want, if sickness be thy lot,
And thou require a soothing friend,
Forget me not, forget me not!

—*Amelia Opie*

$\mathcal{S}$he is probably by this time as tired of me, as I am of her; but as she is too polite and I am too civil to say so, our letters are still as frequent and affectionate as ever, and our Attachment as firm and sincere as when it first commenced.

—*Jane Austen*

*F*or there is no friend like a sister
    In calm or stormy weather;
To cheer one on the tedious way,
To fetch one if one goes astray,
To lift one if one totters down,
To strengthen whilst one stands.

—*Christina Georgina Rossetti*

baby sister is nicer than a goat. You'll get used to her.

—*Lynne Alpern and Esther Blumenfeld*

$\mathcal{M}$y sister and I may have been crafted of the same genetic clay, baked in the same uterine kiln, but we were disparate species, doomed never to love each other except blindly.

—*Judith Kelman*

$\mathcal{S}$weet is the voice of a sister in the season of sorrow, and wise is the counsel of those who love us.

—*Benjamin Disraeli,*
Earl of Beaconsfield

*I*f ever hapless woman had a
cause
To breathe her plaints into the open air,
And never suffer inward grief to pause,
Or seek her sorrow-shaken soul's repair:
Then I, for I have lost my only brother,
Whose like this age can scarcely yield
another.

—*Mary Sidney Herbert*

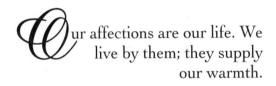

ur affections are our life. We
live by them; they supply
our warmth.

— *William Ellery Channing*

*Y*ou think I love you from
complaisance and ask
you to visit me from
politeness. I don't. I love you
because I love you.

—*Louise Honorine de Choiseul*

$\mathcal{M}$y sister four years older simply existed for me because I had to sleep in the same room with her. Besides, it is natural not to care about a sister, not when she is four years older and grinds her teeth at night.

—*Gertrude Stein*

*W*e are sisters. We will always
be sisters. Our differences
may never go away, but neither, for me,
will our song.

—*Nancy Kelton*

$\mathcal{W}$e are each other's reference
point at our turning points.

— *Elizabeth Fishel*

$\mathcal{I}$f you don't understand how a woman could both love her sister dearly and want to wring her neck at the same time, then you were probably an only child.

—*Linda Sunshine*

*W*inter, spring, summer or fall
All you have to do is call
And I'll be there,
You've got a friend.

—Carole King

friend is one who knows all
about you and likes you
anyway.

—*Katherine Mansfield*

To have a loving relationship with a sister is not simply to have a buddy or a confidant—it is to have a soulmate for life.

— *Victoria Secunda*

I wish dolphin were by my side, in a bath, bright blue, with her tail curled. But then I've always been in love with her since I was a green eyed brat under the nursery table, and so shall remain in my extreme senility.

—*Virginia Woolf,*
of her sister

ministering angel shall my
sister be.

— *William Shakespeare*

$\mathcal{W}$e'd fall asleep holding on to
each other's hair.

*—Ashley Judd,
of her sister Wynonna*

*T*he essence of true friendship is
to make allowance's for
another's little lapses.

—David Storey

I must tell you that I have had a whole field of garlic planted for your benefit, so that when you come, we may be able to have plenty of your favorite dishes!

—*Beatrice D'Este,*
in a letter to her sister, Isabella

[*E*mily's] love was poured out on Anne, as Charlotte's was on her. But the affection among all the three was stronger than either death or life.

—*Elizabeth Gaskell,*
of the Brontë sisters

*M*y Sister! My Sister! If a name
Dearer and purer were, it
should be thine

— *George Noel Gordon,*
Lord Byron

$\mathcal{I}$ looked on her as a mother, and I worshipped the ground she trod on. She would look after me and comfort me and be firm when I had my tantrums. I loved her as a child and I loved her all my life.

—*Mary Ashley,*
of her sister Edwina

$\mathcal{L}$eave thou thy sister when she
prays,
Her early Heaven, her happier views;
Nor thou with shadow'd hint confuse
A life that leads melodious days
Her faith thro' form is pure as thine,
Her hands are quicker into good:
O sacred be the flesh and blood
To which she links a truth divine!

—*Alfred,*
Lord Tennyson

$\mathcal{K}$eep love in your heart. A life
without it is like a garden
when the flowers are dead. The
consciousness of loving and being loved
brings a warmth and richness to a life
that nothing else can bring.

—*Oscar Wilde*

*M*y sister Emily loved the moors. Flowers brighter than the rose bloomed in the blackest of the heath for her; out of a sullen hollow in a livid hill-side her mind could make an Eden. She found in the bleak solitude many and dear delights; and not the least and best loved was — liberty.

—*Charlotte Brontë*

I cannot deny that, now I am without your company I feel not only that I am deprived of a very dear sister, but that I have lost half of myself.

—*Beatrice D'Este*

$\mathcal{K}$risten and Katy are my youngest sisters. Although we have different fathers, I don't think of them as half-sisters at all. They are complete sisters in all senses of the world, unstinting in their teasing and devotion. . . . And if they were not my sisters, I'd want to be their friend.

—*Brett Butler*

$\mathcal{A}$s for the relationship between Paola and myself, from our earliest childhood up to today—a period spanning over three quarters of a century—it has been characterized by an intensity of affection so great as to have created, especially while we were children, a sort of barrier against the intrusion of third parties.

—*Rita Levi-Montalcini*

Oh! call my brother back to me!
I cannot play alone;
The summer comes with flower and
bee —
Where is my brother gone?

—Felicia Dorothea Hemans

*Y*ou can't think how I depend
on you, and when you're
not there the color goes
out of my life.

—*Virginia Woolf,*
to her sister

*W*herever I turn, in the house or out-of-doors, I seem to see your face before my eyes, and when I find myself deceived, and realize that you are really gone, you will understand how sore my distress has been — nay, how great it still is.

—Beatrice D'Este

*T*he key to my locked spirit is
your laughing mouth.

—*Nur Jahan*

I learned to look at her, and as a result, to see her for the first time. I began to love her. The whole process took about one summer. It's curious, but there is perhaps no one in the world as dear to me as Mimi.

—*Joan Baez,*
of her sister

$\mathcal{F}$rom our earliest moments . . . we
wanted nothing but each other . . .
She was the soul of my soul. . . .

—*Fanny Burney,*
of her sister

She is a beautiful girl . . . I think
she will write *something great
one of these days.* . . . I think perhaps one
reason why other girls are not more
attractive may be because I have been so
much with Louisa who is so
uncommonly interesting & funny that
beside her, other girls seem
commonplace.

—Anna Alcott,
of her sister Louisa May

$\mathcal{I}$ think that I had an attachment for my elder sister and that she was very fond and proud of me. I remember that between ten and twelve I felt unhappy before going to sleep and Emilie was kind enough to move her couch near to mine and I went to sleep holding her hand.

—*Melanie Klein*

*A*s for Louisa, I really think that in my life I never knew or heard of anything equal to the sweetness and gentleness of her disposition. She is indeed as yet quite an angel.

—Emily Lennox,
of her sister

*B*ack in 1979, when I was making my first tentative inroads into the music business, my sister Alice gave me—of all things—a toilet seat cover. On it were monogrammed the words, "The Twinkle." She promised that if I ever made it big, she'd give me another one labeled "The Star." But she hasn't yet.

—*Reba McEntire*

$\mathcal{T}$here was no one ever like her.
She was something
wonderful and beautiful, and so simple
and thought so little of herself. I don't
think she ever knew how much she was
to me . . .

—*Constance Gore-Booth,*
of her sister

$\mathcal{F}$rom the time we were little girls I always felt like I was Robin's protector. I can remember when we were small, Robin didn't like milk. But she would drink it if I tasted it for her first. We've just always had this understanding that I would always look out for her.

—*Stephanie Givens,*
of her sister

*I*n thee my soul shall own
combined
The sister and the friend.
If from my eyes by thee detained
The wanderer cross the seas,
No more thy love shall soothe, as friend,
No more as sister please.

—*Catherine Killigrew*

I feel basically very motherly toward my sisters. That hasn't changed at all. If I thought they were doing something drastically wrong with their lives, I would advise them about it.

—*Joanna Simon*

$\mathcal{S}$isterhood is to friendship what an arranged marriage is to romance. You are thrown together for life, no questions asked (until later), no chance of escape. And if you are lucky, you find love despite the confinement.

—*Lisa Grunwald*

We have supported each other through good times and bad, for richer or poorer, in sickness and health, yet we have all gone our separate way, each standing on her own two feet and living her personal life according to her singular beliefs. I admire all three of them for the good women they are — both in mind and spirit.

—Dianne Lennon,
of her sisters

*T*he best thing about having a
sister was that I always had
a friend.

—*Cali Rae Turner*

There is no substitute for the comfort supplied by the utterly taken-for-granted relationship.

—*Iris Murdoch*

*G*iving is a necessity
sometimes . . .
more urgent,
indeed, than having.

—*Margaret Lee Runbeck*

$\mathcal{M}$y sisters knew I loved them, but I was very closemouthed about it. I didn't say it enough, because it was hard for me. But let me tell you, if you have sisters still living, you'd better hug them. You'll regret it if they go and you didn't get a chance to express that feeling. And they'd probably have been waiting for it. I know my sisters were waiting for me.

—*Patti LaBelle,*
of her three sisters

The recommended daily requirement for hugs is: four per day for survival, eight per day for maintenance, and twelve per day for growth.

—*Virginia Satir*

$\mathcal{S}$isterly love is, of all sentiments,
the most abstract.

— *Ugo Betti*

$\mathcal{A}$lthough I see my three sisters less often than I do my chosen friends, and in many ways I have less in common with them, I know that if anything happened to them, I would feel as if I had lost a limb.

—*Annie Gottlieb*

*H*er presence makes the room warm and alive for me. I want to be where she is. It is not a very conscious feeling—just a vague discontent with the places she is not. There is more life where she is. I get up and follow her when she moves from one room to another as one might unconsciously follow a moving patch of sunlight in a room.

—*Anne Morrow Lindbergh,*
of her sister

There are two ways of spreading
light: to be
The candle or the mirror that reflects it.

—*Edith Wharton*

I have always loved my sister's voice. It is clear and light, a voice without seasons, like bells over a green city or snowfall on the roots of orchids.

— *Pat Conroy*

$\mathcal{H}$aving a sister is like having a best friend you can't get rid of. You know whatever you do, they'll still be there.

—*Amy Li*

I always felt that the great high privilege, relief, and comfort of friendship was that one had to explain nothing.

—*Katherine Mansfield*

$\mathcal{A}$s young children, my sisters and I were close. I enjoyed being the oldest, showing them around, protecting them. When a bully who sat across from Susan at the schoolroom table kicked her legs black-and-blue, I beat him up in the playground.

—*Patricia Ireland*

*T*herefore friends should quarrel to strengthen their attachment, and offend each other for the pleasure of being reconciled.

—*Maria Edgeworth*

I rather think I'm more nearly attached to you than sisters should be. Why is it I never stop thinking of you, even when walking in the marsh this afternoon. . . . If you notice a dancing light on the water that is me. The light kisses your nose, then your eyes, and you can't rub it off; my darling honey how I adore you, and lord knows I can't say what it means to me to come into the room and find you sitting there.

—Virginia Woolf,
in a letter to her sister

When I have Gladys in my arms and press her against my heart I know what love is, at least I know how it feels to love tenderly, truly, deeply, sincerely.

—*Gertrude Vanderbilt Whitney,*
of her sister

$\mathcal{N}$o soul is desolate as long as there is a human being for whom it can feel trust and reverence.

— *George Eliot*

*Y*ou would laugh, or you would cry, perhaps both, to see us sit together looking at each other with long and rueful faces, & saying how do you do? & then we fall a crying & say we will be better on the morrow. . . .

—*Mary Anne Lamb,*
of her brother Charles

*H*ow do people make it through
life without a sister?

—*Sara Corpening*

*N*either one of us ever married and we've lived together most all of our lives, and probably know each other better than any two human beings on Earth. After so long, we are in some ways like one person. She is my right arm.

—*Sadie Delany,*
of her sister

"My dear Jane!" exclaimed Elizabeth, "you are too good. Your sweetness and disinterestedness are really angelic; I do not know what to say to you. I feel as if I had never done you justice, or loved you as you deserve."

—*Jane Austen*

The best way of thinking about attachment, in my view, is to see it as the outcome of an interaction between two people, each of whom contributes to the quality of the relationship.

—*Sandra Scarr*

$\mathcal{B}$etween sisters, often, the child's cry never dies down. "Never leave me," it says; "do not abandon me."

—*Louise Bernikow*

The love that grew with us from our cradles never knew diminuition from time or distance. Other ties were formed, but they did not supersede or weaken this. Death tore away at all that was mortal and perishable, but this tie he could not sunder.

—*Charolette Elizabeth Tonna*

*W*hatever you do they will love you; even if they don't love you they are connected to you till you die. You can be boring and tedious with sisters, whereas you have to put on a good face with friends.

—*Deborah Moggach*

$\mathcal{I}$ do not expect or want you to be otherwise than you are, I love you for the good that is in you, and look for no change.

—*Mary Anne Lamb*

Sisters is probably the most competitive relationship within the family, but once sisters are grown, it becomes the strongest relationship.

—*Margaret Mead*

*Y*ou know full well as I do the
value of sister's affections to
each other; there is nothing
like it in the world.

—*Charlotte Brontë*

Words
That
Connect
Us

*T*here can be no situation in life in which the conversation of my dear sister will not administer some comfort to me.

—*Lady Mary Wortley Montagu*

There's no vocabulary
For love within the
family, love that's lived in
But not looked at, love within the light
of which
All else is seen, the love within which
All other love finds speech.
This love is silent.

— *T. S. Eliot*

$\mathcal{I}$ thank you and bless you dearest Henrietta and Arabel . . . my own dearest kindest sisters! . . . My thoughts cling to you all, and will not leave their hold. Dearest Henrietta and Arabel let me be as ever and for ever.

—*Elizabeth Barrett Browning,*
in a letter to her sisters

*Y*our conversation is a spring
that never fails, never
overflows.

—*Mary Russell Mitford*

𝒴ou were being Isadora; I was
being you.
Did I know that I'd grow
to say:
You've got me flying, I'm flying . . .
You inspired a sister song . . .

Holly Near

By now we know and anticipate one another so easily, so deeply, we unthinkingly finish each other's sentences, and often speak in code. No one else knows what I mean so exquisitely, painfully well; no one else knows so exactly what to say, to fix me.

—*Joan Frank*

*T*hat is one great difference
between us. Compliments
always take you by surprise, and *me*
never.

—*Jane Austen*

*B*less you, my darling, and remember you are always in the heart—oh tucked so close there is no chance of escape—of your sister.

—*Katherine Mansfield*

*D*ear Sister,
Your
kind letter I receiv'd today
and am greatly rejoiced to [hear] you
are all so well. . . . I daily count the days
between this and the time I may
probably see you . . . I would give a
great deal only to know I was within ten
miles of you if I could not see you.

Mary Smith Cranch,
in a letter to her sister Abigail Adams

$\mathcal{M}$y tears keep all alive.

—*Marceline Desbordes-Valmore,*
in a letter to her sister Cecile

This is the iron age. Grief, luxury, poverty, make men wild. For hearts as warm as ours, it is cold.

—*Marceline Desbordes-Valmore,*
in a letter to her sister Cecile

*E*very smart
Is eased in
telling.

—*Georgiana Goddard King*

$\mathcal{L}$etters are venerable; and the telephone valiant, for the journey is a lonely one, and if bound together by notes and telephones we went in company, perhaps—who knows?—we might talk by the way.

—*Virginia Woolf*

I am often with you, my dear Berthe. In my thoughts I follow you about in your studio, and wish that I could escape, were it only for a quarter of an hour, to breathe that air in which we lived for many years.

—*Edma Pontillion,*
in a letter to her sister

By secrecy I mean you both want the habit of telling each other at the moment everything that happens, —where you go —and what you do —that free communication of letters and opinions, just as they arise, as [my brother] and I do, and which is after all the only groundwork for friendship. . . .

—*Mary Anne Lamb*

*G*ood communication is
stimulating as black
coffee, and just as
hard to sleep after.

—*Anne Morrow Lindbergh*

*M*any a time we walk't together
& with discorce have pleasd
each other.

—*Anna Thompson Hayden*

How are you my sweet Tanyanka? I am often sad that you are not here with me. In spite of the fact that life is simply wonderful, things would be better still if I could hear your sweet nightingale voice, if I could sit and gossip with you as we used to do. . . . I haven't yet got quite used to things. It still seems strange to me that when I am at Yasnaya I am at home. . . .

—*Sonya Tolstoy,*
in a letter to her sister

$\mathcal{W}$hat are the wild waves saying
Sister, the whole day long?

—*Joseph Edwards Carpenter*

$\mathcal{F}$or as long as I can remember, Anne wanted to be a novelist. Her head was filled with stories to tell. She came home and wrote and it got her through every experience. She's as thorough a writer in her heart and soul as anyone I've ever met.

— Tamara O'Brien,
of her sister Anne Rice

$\mathcal{L}$istening to my sister sing has been one of the greatest gifts of my life.

—*Norman Buckley*

I will not forget the blessings that sweeten Life. One of those is the prospect I have before me of meeting my dear sister soon, I hope in health and spirits. A strong imagination is said to be a refuge from sorrow, and a kindly solace for a feeling heart.

—*Abigail Adams,*
in a letter to her sister

felt it a shelter to speak to you.

—*Emily Dickinson*

There is more in parting than we thought when we used to talk so quietly about it. I only thought of the actual loss of your company . . . and forgot the terrible feeling of regret with which one looks back to almost every incident of our lives, regret that it is all past and sorrow at the countless things I was wrong in: things seem so pleasant when we look back at them.

—Rachel Henning,
in a letter to her sister

You may choose your word like
a connoisseur,
And polish it up with art,
But the word that sways, and stirs, and
stays,
Is the word that comes from the heart.

—*Ella Wheeler Wilcox*

$\mathcal{M}$y dearest Ba
Would you
deign to read this little letter as a pledge
of my affection to you; I should be glad
if your genius would allow me a little of
your poetic taste, but as the muse turns
her back upon poor me, and as I believe
you know I try to do it as well I can . . .
may you be the happiest of the happy!

—*Henrietta Moulton-Barrett,*
in a letter to her sister Elizabeth

We are not *only* sisters. It is amazing and sort of a doubly strong association to be linked instinctively (and by environment, early life, etc.) and by one's desire and reason. It is a rare relationship. I feel as though you have leaned down and lifted me up to where you were so many times.

—*Anne Morrow Lindbergh,*
in a letter to her sister

Someone to tell it to is one of the fundamental needs of human beings.

—*Miles Franklin*

*J*ust a line sister dear—Have been
very sick & suffered— & they
say I am better, but still at death's
door—Have the best attention &
watching—send *best* love & God bless
you.

—*Walt Whitman,*
in one of his last letters to his sister Hannah

i f i cud ever write a poem as beautiful
as u, little 2/yr/old/brotha,
poetry wud go out of bizness

—*Sonia Sanchez*

$\mathcal{S}$hut these odious books up,
                         brother—
They made you quite another
Thing from what you used to be;
Once you liked to play with me . . .

—*Mary Anne Lamb*

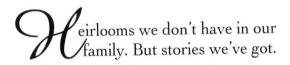

$\mathcal{H}$eirlooms we don't have in our family. But stories we've got.

—*Rose Chernin*

*W*hat strange creatures brothers are! You would not write to each other but upon the most urgent necessity in the world; and when obliged to take up a pen and say that such a horse is ill, or such a relation is dead, it is done in the fewest possible words. You have but one style among you. I know it perfectly. Henry, who is in every other respect exactly what a brother should be . . . has never yet turned the page in a letter; and very often it is nothing more than — 'Dear Mary, I am just arrived. Bath seems full and everything as usual. Yours sincerely.' That is the true manly style; that is a complete brothers letter.

—*Jane Austen*

*O*nce in a while Ann and I write letters. "My begonias are blooming," she said in one, "and I don't even *like* them." Only between ourselves and a very few others dare we expose such examples of ugly ingratitude.

—*Jane Howard*

$\mathcal{H}$ow can we communicate love? I think three things are involved: we must reach out to a person, make contact. We must listen with the heart, be sensitive to the other's needs. We must respond in a language that the person can understand. Many of us do all the talking. We must learn to listen and to keep on listening.

—*Princess Pale Moon*

$\mathcal{R}$emember my unalterable
maxim, where we love,
we always have something to say.

—*Lady Mary Wortley Montagu*

*B*ut now you have a horrid cold,
And in an ugly night cap you
are rolled,
Which spoils the nat'ral beauty of your face,
Where dimples play in every cunning place;
I wish you would so nicely run,
And then we would have merry fun,
But o'er the fire you poking sit,
As if for nothing you were fit. . . .
Indeed I hope you'll soon get better . . .

— *Elizabeth Barrett Browning,*
in a letter to her sister Henrietta

I hope we may all succeed in pleasing you on your birthday; we shall all try to do so, as we have tried to make you happy on all your birthdays but I cannot expect that my little letter can give you as much pleasure, as your beautiful verses gave me and wish I could write verses for your sake, but I love you as dearly . . .

—*Henrietta Moulton-Barrett,*
in a letter to her sister Elizabeth

eaching my sister to read, write,
and count gave me, from the
age of six onwards, a sense of pride in
my own efficiency. . . . When I started to
change ignorance into knowledge, when
I started to impress truths upon a virgin
mind, I felt I was at last creating
something real.

—*Simone de Beauvoir*

*W*henever we went on walks we'd sit in the long grass on the side of the hills and Sylvia would start off on these beautiful stories. . . . These stories would go on and on. I was enthralled.

—Norma Warner, of her sister

*W*hat a lot we lost when we
stopped writing letters!
You can't re-read a phone call.

—*Liz Carpenter*

I miss you so all the time, my dear sisters! I never before felt so deeply how much I love you, and how very much I depend on you. The thought of being so widely separated from you was almost unbearable; particularly at the time little Mathilde was on the way, and I didn't yet know where I should be able to get help.

—Julie Scramm,
in a letter to her sisters

I assure you I am as tired of writing long letters as you can be. What a pity that one should still be so fond of receiving them.

—*Jane Austen,*
in a letter to her sister Cassandra

$\mathcal{W}$orldly possessions fade away,
but this refuge remains
immutable.

—*Marceline Desbordes-Valmore,*
in a letter to her brother

*N*ow that she must see for Mary as well as for herself, Laura saw everything. . . . Necessity sharpened her perceptions, and she struggled for words to express them. . . . She felt how poor words were for telling what she had seen. She tried to find the right words, but there were some things that couldn't be fitted into words.

—*Donald Zochert,*
of Laura Ingalls Wilder and her sister Mary

And be my sister blessed in
every spot
In every station and in every lot
Long may she live with sweet
contentment here
For ever cherished and for ever dear

—*Elizabeth Barrett Browning,*
in a letter to her sister Henrietta

Communication is a continual balancing act, juggling the conflicting needs for intimacy and independence. To survive in the world, we have to act in concert with each other, but to survive as ourselves, rather than simply as cogs in the wheel, we have to act alone.

—*Deborah Tannen*

[*My* sisters and I] have dinner-table debates about whether it's better to establish a career first or plan a family first. But the discussions are really for fun, since we're all so different we couldn't have imitated each other if we'd tried.

—*Kathy Sparkman*

*S*ometimes I think I know
everything there is to
know about my sisters but this isn't true.
I talk about them too much to strangers
and worry afterwards that I've left out
everything that is important.

—*Gillian Mears*

Family Life

[Our family is] a wonderfully messy arrangement, in which relationships overlap, underlie, support, and oppose one another. It didn't always come together easily nor does it always stay together easily. It has held together, often out of shared memories and hopes, sometimes out of the lure of my sisters' cooking, and sometimes out of sheer stubbornness. And like the world itself, our family is renewed by each baby.

—*Marge Kennedy*

If the family were a fruit, it would be an orange, a circle of sections, held together but separable—each segment distinct.

—*Letty Cottin Pogrebin*

$\mathcal{T}$he informality of family life is a
blessed condition that allows
us to become our best while looking
our worst.

—Marge Kennedy

*F*ather, Mother and Me,
    Sister and Auntie say
All the people like us are we,
And everyone else is They.

—*Rudyard Kipling*

A gorgeous example of denial is the story about the little girl who was notified that a baby . . . sister was on the way. She listened in thoughtful silence, then raised her gaze from her mother's belly to her eyes and said, "Yes, but who will be the new baby's mommy?"

—*Judith Viorst*

My earliest recollection is of the third-story room my parents occupied in that house. Somehow I was in the room—I had crawled under the bed when the doctor arrived and perhaps had fallen asleep there. I heard a cry. It was the first cry of my new sister, Alyce. I peeked out. There was the doctor and there was his black bag. Long after I should have known better, I believed that Alyce had been fetched in that black bag.

—*Marian Anderson*

*O*nly a sister can compare the sleek body that now exists with the chubby body hidden underneath. Only a sister knows about former pimples, failing math, and underwear kicked under the bed.

—*Laura Tracy*

*L*iving with a sister is easier than moving in with a friend. When your new roommate is not a family member, you both act like nervous newlyweds.

—*Jeanie Pyun*

$\mathcal{W}$e are born into them, marry into them, even create them among the people we love. They come large and extended . . . or small and nuclear. But whatever their size or wherever they live, strong families give us the nurturance and strength we need in order to survive.

—*Andrea Davis*

$\mathcal{M}$y Aunt & my mother were wholly unlike you and your sister, yet in some degree theirs is the secret history I believe of all sisters-in-law. . . .

—*Mary Anne Lamb*

*A*ll I can gather from your clear, & I have no doubt, faithful history of Maltese politics, is, that . . . your sister in law is pretty much like what all sisters in law have been since the first happy invention of the happy marriage state.

—*Mary Anne Lamb*

*K*eep what is worth keeping—
And with the breath of
kindness
Blow the rest away.

—*Dinah Mulock Craik*

Our daily existence requires both closeness and distance, the wholeness of self, the wholeness of intimacy.

—*Judith Viorst*

*D*o not be cool towards a close relative on account of some small quarrel; do not forget an old act of kindness because of a recent dispute.

Mr. Tut-Tut,
translated by Lin Yutang

_K_indness and intelligence don't always deliver us from the pitfalls and traps: there are always failures of love, of will, of imagination. There is no way to take the danger out of human relationships.

—_Barbara Grizzuti Harrison_

O! men with sisters dear,
O! men with mothers
and wives!
It is not linen you're wearing out,
But human creatures' lives!

— *Thomas Hood*

$\mathcal{F}$amily quarrels are bitter things. They don't go according to any rules. They're not like aches or wounds; they're more like splits in the skin that won't heal because there's not enough material.

—*F. Scott Fitzgerald*

$\mathcal{W}$e were like ill-sorted animals
tied to a common tethering
post.

—*Jessica Mitford,*
of her family

$\mathcal{W}$hatever brawls disturb the
street
There should be peace at home.

—Isaac Watts

The more you judge, the less you love.

—Honoré de Balzac

*I*f you have only one smile in you, give it to the people you love. Don't be surly at home, then go out into the street and start grinning "Good morning" at total strangers.

—*Maya Angelou*

*T*reat your friends like family and
your family like friends.

—Michele Slung

If the family were a boat, it would be a canoe that makes no progress unless everyone paddles.

—*Letty Cottin Pogrebin*

*W*here we love is home,
    Home that our feet
        may leave,
    but not our hearts.

—*Oliver Wendell Holmes*

It is very difficult to live among people you love and hold back from offering them advice.

—*Anne Tyler*

*E*ven when you think people are wrong, it is easy to tell when they are right. When they are right about something you are trying very hard to hide from others and yourself, you know they are right because you want to kill them.

—*Candice Bergen*

*A*mong the most disheartening
and dangerous of . . .
advisors, you will often find those
closest to you, your dear friends,
members of your own family, perhaps,
loving, anxious, and knowing nothing
whatever.

—*Minnie Maddern Fiske*

The true secret of giving advice is, after you have honestly given it, to be perfectly indifferent whether it is taken or not, and never persist in trying to set people right.

—*Hannah Whitall Smith*

It is curious to see how a self-willed, haughty girl, who sets her father and mother all at defiance, and cannot be managed by anybody, at once finds her master in a baby. Her sister's child will strike the rock and set all her affection flowing.

—*Charles Buxton*

I am the family face;
Flesh perishes, I
live on,
Projecting trait and trace
Through time to times anon,
And leaping from place to place
Over oblivion.

— *Thomas Hardy*

*F*amily traits, like murder, will [come] out. Nature has but so many molds.

—*Louise Imogen Guiney*

*F*amily faces are magic mirrors.
Looking at people who
belong to us, we see the past, present
and future.

—*Gail Lumet Buckley*

In our family, as far as we are concerned, we were born and what happened before that is a myth.

—*V. S. Pritchett*

$\mathcal{W}$hat families have in common
the world round is that they
are the place where people learn who
they are and how to be that way.

—*Jean Illsley Clarke*

Happy or unhappy, families are all mysterious. We have only to imagine how differently we would be described—and will be, after our deaths—by each of the family members who believe they know us.

—*Gloria Steinem*

Sisters are always drying their hair.
Locked into rooms alone,
They pose at the mirror, shoulders bare,
Trying this way and that their hair,
Or fly importunate down the stair
To answer the telephone.

—*Phyllis McGinley*

$\mathcal{W}$e do not discuss the members
of our family to their faces.

—Ivy Compton-Burnett

$\mathcal{I}$ am convinced that more unpleasant feelings are created in families, by these false delicacies, and managements, and hints, and go-between friends by courtesy, than ever would have been caused by the parties speaking directly to one another, and telling the plain truth about their thoughts and wishes.

—*Maria Edgeworth*

She took to telling the truth; she said that she was forty-two and five months. It may have been pleasing to the angels, but her elder sister was not gratified.

—*Saki [H. H. Munro]*

*F*amily life is not a computer program that runs on its own; it needs continual input from everyone.

—*Neil Kurshan*

*S*oup is a lot like a family. Each
ingredient enhances the
others; each batch has its own
characteristics; and it needs time to
simmer to reach full flavor.

—*Marge Kennedy*

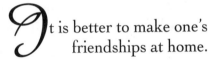

𝒥t is better to make one's
friendships at home.

—*Plutarch*

$\mathcal{T}$he greatest thing in family life is to take a hint when a hint is intended—and not to take a hint when a hint isn't intended.

—*Robert Frost*

The only rock I know that stays steady, the only institution I know that works is the family.

—*Lee Iacocca*

$\mathcal{F}$amily jokes, though rightly cursed
by strangers, are the bond that
keeps most families alive.

—*Stella Benson*

The family the soul wants is a felt network of relationship, an evocation of certain types of interconnection that grounds, roots, and nestles.

— *Thomas More*

*Y*ou think you have a handle on
God, the Universe, and the
Great White Light until
you go home for Thanksgiving. In an
hour, you realize how far you've got to
go and who is the real turkey.

—*Shirley MacLaine*

One of the things that has contributed to our survival has been a strong family background. I think the fact that we are family has helped us stay together, to deal and cope with one another's problems. When one of us gets a little weak, there are others around who can strengthen her.

—*Debbie Sledge,*
of her sisters

The family. We are a strange little band of characters trudging through life sharing diseases and toothpaste, coveting one another's desserts, hiding shampoo, borrowing money, locking each other out of rooms, inflicting pain and kissing to heal it in the same instant, loving, laughing, defending, and trying to figure out the common thread that bound us all together.

—*Erma Bombeck*

Siblings

$\mathcal{A}$ sibling may be the keeper of one's identity, the only person with the keys to one's unfettered, more fundamental self.

—*Marian Sandmaier*

$\mathcal{M}$ore than Santa Claus, your sister knows when you've been bad and good.

—*Linda Sunshine*

*O*ur brothers and sisters bring us face to face with our former selves and remind us how intricately bound up we are in each other's lives.

—*Jane Mersky Leder*

Oh! yet a little while
May I behold in
thee what I was once,
My dear, dear Sister!

— *William Wordsworth*

$\mathcal{M}$y sister Georgina was born the day after my own birthday, when I was nine. I always felt as if she was my own child. I could immediately cuddle her, and I could dress her up as well. Dolls weren't my cup of tea—I always had teddy bears—but she was my doll and I absolutely adored her.

—*Antoinette Sibley*

*h*ow sister gazed at sister
reaching through
mirrored pupils
back to the mother

—*Adrienne Rich*

We have to divide mother love with our brothers and sisters. Our parents can help us cope with the loss of our dream of absolute love. But they cannot make us believe that we haven't lost it.

—*Judith Viorst*

*O*ft I see her when I sleep,
  And her kiss feel on my
          brow;
But when morning comes, I weep,
  Just as you do, Sister, now.

—*Marguerite Blessington,*
of their mother

*S*isters define their rivalry in terms
of competition for the gold cup
of parental love. It is never perceived as
a cup which runneth over, rather a finite
vessel from which the more one sister
drinks, the less is left for the others.

—*Elizabeth Fishel*

*T*ogether we look like our
mother. Her same eyes,
her same mouth, open in surprise to see,
at last, her long-cherished wish.

—*Amy Tan*

It's a great comfort to have an artistic sister.

—*Louisa May Alcott*

I have nothing against
undertakers
personally. It's just that I wouldn't want
one to bury my sister.

—*Jessica Mitford*

A sister can be seen as someone who is both ourselves and very much not ourselves—a special kind of double.

— *Toni A. H. McNaron*

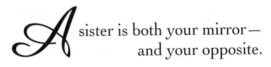

$\mathcal{A}$ sister is both your mirror—
and your opposite.

—*Elizabeth Fishel*

$\mathcal{E}$ven when [my sister and I] are separated by continents, we are moving through time in parallel tracks.

—*Kennedy Fraser*

*T*hey are, and yet they are
not, two.

—*Katherine Fowler Philips*

$\mathcal{S}$he looks up to me and tries to copy everything that I do, which is partly really adorable and partly kind of annoying. Sometimes I get to the point where I just want to say "Okay, please leave me alone for a while now." But Christina still follows me around.

—*Dominique Moceanu,*
of her sister

*S*isters examine each other so they can have a map for how they should behave.

—*Michael D. Kahn*

*E*ven the conjugal tie is beneath the fraternal. Children of the same family, the same blood, with the same first associations and habits, have some means of enjoyment in their power, which no subsequent connection can supply.

—*Jane Austen*

*C*omparison is a death knell to
sibling harmony.

—*Elizabeth Fishel*

$\mathcal{G}$oing down the stairs now
behind your anxious,
baby steps
I want to pick you up and carry you
or launch you down the banister
as you did me
in this house
when we were children together

—*Mary Dorcey*

$\mathcal{T}$he difference between us is I will
shop for something expensive
but just buy one thing . . . Whereas Alex
will buy 150 shirts and 150 cardigans . . .
but they sit there and just accumulate
and accumulate.

—*Marie-Chantal Miller*

used to get on Phylicia's nerves
when I was a little girl.

—*Debbie Allen,*
of her sister Phylicia Rashad

$\mathcal{I}$t was worse than that. Whenever she came around me, I got into trouble.

—*Phylicia Rashad,*
of her sister Debbie Allen

To most people, my sister and I didn't seem to have much in common; but I knew . . . that we were remarkably alike.

—*Kathleen Norris*

*A*ll three sisters had the same
high-bridged noses . . . I
pored over these pictures, intrigued by
the idea of the triplicate, identical noses.
I did not have a sister myself, then, and
the mystique of sisterhood was potent
for me.

—*Margaret Atwood*

*I*f we are the younger, we may envy the older. If we are the older, we may feel that the younger is always being indulged. In other words, no matter what position we hold in family order of birth, we can prove beyond a doubt that we're being gypped.

—*Judith Viorst*

We were born 10 minutes apart, Adrian first. She always said she was the real baby, and I was a kind of backup.

—Adair Lara,
of her sister

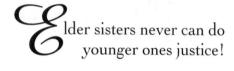

*E*lder sisters never can do
younger ones justice!

—*Charlotte M. Yonge*

*M*y sister and I are 11 years apart, so basically she was like having a baby of my own. I diapered her, fed her, and was there like a proud parent for every step of her development.

—*Melissa Gilbert, of her sister Sara*

I grew up with a sister four years older than I who's very pretty, the quintessential California girl. I had been this bean pole, and didn't think that I was anything special.

—*Molly Ringwald*

*W*alking down the street with Mauryne was an exercise in attraction. . . . She pretended not to notice the havoc she caused on the streets. Stubby and shapeless in my shorts and braids, I was dazzled and proud that this beautiful creature was my big sister.

—*Shirlee Taylor Haizlip*

*N*ever praise a sister to a sister,
in hope of your compliments
reaching the proper ears.

—Rudyard Kipling

*B*ut what about a sister? What is a sister born for? My sister was born to be the rock of our family . . . She was the one who showed me what women of faith look like; she put skin and flesh and life on those old stories of women in the Bible. She taught me how to live. She made me proud of our family.

— Caroline Burns

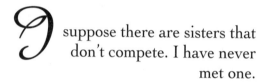

suppose there are sisters that don't compete. I have never met one.

—*Lisa Grunwald*

*I*f I *never* in my life meet anyone else, I have been happier than anyone who ever lived in knowing her: It must be like being in love. I am never envious of her—her writing, her music, anything. I know how wonderful she is. Nothing is too good for her. . . .

—*Anne Morrow Lindbergh,
of her sister Constance*

My oldest sister Mary, possessed . . . an innate charm and gentleness. She could do anything along domestic lines—embroidery, dress making, tailoring, cooking; she could concoct the most delicious and unusual foods, and mix delicate pastries. But she was also an expert at upholstering, carpentry, painting, roofing with shingles or with thatch. When Mary was in the house, we never had to send for a plumber.

—*Margaret Sanger*

*A*dvances towards heroism in
her sister made Elinor feel
equal to anything herself.

—*Jane Austen*

$\mathcal{S}$he is to me a never-ending source
of astonishment and admiration.
And I never cease to wonder at my luck
in having for my sister the woman who,
more than any other woman in America,
possesses all the qualities of greatness.

—Dorothy Gish,
of her sister Lillian

*W*hat surprised me was that within a family, the voices of sisters as they're talking are virtually always the same.

—*Elizabeth Fishel*

$\mathcal{M}$y sister! My little sister — I called her that, in spite of the fact that she was two years older than me. . . . I don't think anyone ever regarded me as a child. . . .

— *Greta Garbo*

$\mathcal{I}$n families children tend to take on stock roles, as if there were hats hung up in some secret place, visible only to the children. Each succeeding child takes on that role: the good child, the black sheep, the clown and so forth.

—*Ellen Galinsky*

$\mathcal{M}$y little sister was different. Being perfect was of no interest whatsoever to her. She was a tomboy, she got into scrapes, she hardly ever did what she was told — in short, she never tried to fit anybody else's idea of what her "role" should be.

—*Loni Anderson*

*M*ary had aspirations, confidence, and a will to succeed like no other. While I wallowed in my troubles, making long lists of life's injustices, Mary operated with great practicality and logic.

—*Marti Leimbach*

I knew that my sister always loved me, that she'd always take care of me. But Alline was somehow too slow and quiet for me—I was always up to something, running, moving, doing.

—*Tina Turner*

$\mathcal{M}$y sister is never still. Even as a child she was filled with a restless energy that swung her around flagpoles and into water fountains with parents and grandparents scrambling in her wake.

—*Beth Yahp*

𝒥'm the watcher. I like to observe, and [Joan] very much likes to participate. She likes to be center stage, and I like to sit in the background.

—*Jackie Collins*

*W*hen Dorothy goes swimming, she splashes the ocean into a beautiful gala muss; I just go in swimming. When she dances, there is no tomorrow; when I dance, the trombone always stubbornly reminds me of a director in a bad mood. . . .

—*Lillian Gish,*
of her sister Dorothy

$\mathcal{I}$ was the oldest girl. So, I was helping to raise my brothers and sisters and changing diapers and making lunches and breaking up fights. I speculate that's why I'm comfortable being the bandleader.

—*Joan Osborne*

*H*e had just compunction
enough for having
done nothing for his sisters himself, to
be exceedingly anxious that everybody
else should do a great deal.

—*Jane Austen*

*I*n the history of human affections . . . the least satisfying is the fraternal. Brothers are to sisters what sisters can never be to brothers as objects of engrossing and devoted affection.

—*Harriet Martineau*

She was over six feet tall, too, by an angstrom unit or so. She was heavenly to look at, and graceful, both in and out of the water. She was a sculptress. She was christened "Alice," but she used to deny that she was really an Alice. I agreed. Everybody agreed. Sometime in a dream maybe I will find out what her real name was.

—*Kurt Vonnegut,*
of his sister

$\mathcal{M}$y brothers, the dragonslayers,
capable and strong.

—*Patricia Penton Leimbach*

A man with six sisters, Spider realized with glee, was a rich man—unless he was Greek and had a duty to marry them off.

—*Judith Krantz*

*B*ehold how good and how
pleasant it is for brothers
and sisters to dwell together in unity.

—*The Holy Bible*

The children worked on each
other like two
indestructible pieces of sand paper.

—*Elizabeth Bowen*

*B*irds in their little nests agree
and 'tis a shameful sight
when children of one family
fall out, and chide, and fight.

—*Isaac Watts*

*T*he surest route to breeding jealousy is to compare [siblings]. Since jealousy comes from feeling "less than" another, comparisons only fan the fires.

—*Dorothy Corkville Briggs*

$\mathcal{N}$ever assume one child is always is the victim and the other the aggressor. Remember, no matter how things appear, it takes two to tango. If you look closely enough . . . you will see how the victim subtly provokes the aggressor into attacking.

—*Ron Taffel*

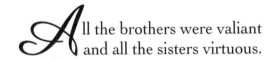

All the brothers were valiant
and all the sisters virtuous.

*From the inscription on the tomb of the Duchess of
Newcastle in Westminster Abbey*

$\mathcal{I}$t seems to me that we have to draw the line in sibling rivalry whenever rivalry goes out of bounds into destructive behavior of a physical or verbal kind. The principle needs to be this: Whatever the reasons for your feelings you will have to find civilized solutions.

—*Selma H. Fraiberg*

$\mathcal{I}$ wrote a long letter to Santa Claus and said that I had been particularly good that year and felt I was quite deserving. I ended with, "I look forward to seeing you." Then I added, "P. S. My turtle died two days ago. I hope my sister's turtle dies too."

—*Francine Clagsbrun*

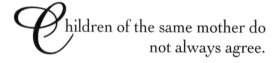

*C*hildren of the same mother do
not always agree.

Nigerian proverb

*M*ama came from a family of many sisters. And she preached to us endlessly about the necessity of living in harmony with one another.

—*bell hooks*

*T*he reason we get along so well is our years of practice. I credit our parents. We weren't allowed to argue. When we did, we were punished. Not one, but two or all three of us, so we'd pull together.

—*Louise Mandrell, of her sisters*

$\mathcal{M}$om sent me to the pantry for flour and I put a half-eaten Milky Way bar on the counter. When I came back, Sheila was eating it. Sheila is the one person on earth who can easily reduce me to the emotions and mentality of a six-year-old.

—*Deborah Perry,*
of her sister

$\mathcal{I}$t is with our brothers and sisters that we learn to love, share, negotiate, start and end fights, hurt others, and save face. The basis of healthy (or unhealthy) connections in adulthood is cast during childhood.

—*Jane Mersky Leder*

*B*ig sisters are the crab grass in
the lawn of life.

—*Charles M. Schultz*

I think if there's no sibling rivalry in a family, there's a lot of denial going on, because you can't help but rub against each other when you're forming who you are.

—*Joanna Kerns*

*C*ompetition is about passion for perfection, and passion for other people who join in this impossible quest.

—*Mariah Burton Nelson*

*K*aterina and I are best friends. The only was we survived in this zoo was to stay close. . . . When I play Katerina I pull harder for her than I do me. I've won all our [tennis] matches, but I've suffered every time.

—*Manuela Maleeva,*
of her sister

$\mathcal{F}$rom the normal irritations of living together, they learn how to assert themselves, defend themselves, compromise. And sometimes, from their envy of each other's special abilities they become inspired to work harder, persist, and achieve.

—*Adele Faber,*
of siblings

$\mathcal{I}$ would have gone through hell
and high water for my sister,
but at the same time, in spite of my
warmest attachment to her, in the
depths of my soul could be found the
lightest bit of envy—that special kind of
envy which we almost unconsciously
cherish toward people very close to us—
those whom we admire very much and
would like to emulate in everything.

—*Sofia Kovalevskaia*

*I*t's just hard because you hold in a lot of stuff. You don't want to outshine; you don't want to upstage, and then you don't want to get too far back in the background, either.

—*June Pointer,*
on family life with a sister

$\mathscr{O}$ne of the best things about
being an adult is the
realization that you can share with your
sister and still have plenty for yourself.

—*Betsy Cohen*

Siblings either learn to accept one another as independent individuals with their own sets of values and behaviors or cling to the shadow of the brother or sister they once knew.

—*Jane Mersky Leder*

It's hard as kids to know what's causing you to feel and react the way you do, but as adults, we worked through a lot of that stuff. Now we're each other's best supporters. No one knows her better than I know her, and vise versa.

—*Joanna Kerns,*
of her sister

$\mathcal{M}$y oldest sister, Alice Lynn Foran . . . is the rock, the one you can call at three in the morning, and she'll always be ready to help in any way.

— *Reba McEntire*

The quickness with which all the "stuff" from childhood can reduce adult siblings to kids again underscores the strong and complex connections between brothers and sisters . . . It doesn't seem to matter how much time has elapsed or how far we've traveled.

—*Jane Mersky Leder*

As siblings we were inextricably bound, even though our connections were loose and frayed . . . And each time we met, we discovered to our surprise and dismay how quickly childhood feelings reappeared . . . No matter how old we got or how often we tried to show another face, reality was filtered through yesterday's memories.

—*Jane Mersky Leder*

*W*hen I look at Martha today, I see parts of myself and parts of my history. She has tested and helped me as no other person has, making me understand my limitations and my capacity for generosity.

—*Barbara Lovenhiem,*
of her sister

I asked her for advice and help. It was a homecoming of sorts. I can still recall the fullness in her voice when she told me how very, very touched she was that at last I was letting her in.

—*Marcia Ann Gillespie,*
of her sister

*Y*our siblings are the only people in the world who know what it's like to have been brought up the way you were.

—*Betsy Cohen*

$\mathcal{B}$essie and I have been together since time began, or so it seems. Bessie is my little sister, only she's not so little. She is 101 years old, and I'm 103. . . . After so long, we are in some ways like one person.

—*Sarah L. Delany*

Sisterhood

$\mathcal{W}$e are thy sisters . . .
Our skins may
differ, but from thee we claim
A sister's privilege and a sister's name.

—*Sarah L. Forten*

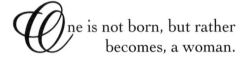

One is not born, but rather becomes, a woman.

— *Simone de Beauvoir*

Beautiful sisters, come high up
to the strongest rocks, we
are all fighting women, heroines,
horsewomen.

—*Edith Södergran*

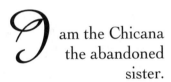

$\mathscr{I}$ am the Chicana
the abandoned
sister.

— *Sylvia Alicia Gonzales*

*S*is, we are destined for something—there is no use thinking otherwise, either good or bad. As for me I would not be surprised to find myself in 20 years from now either in the penitentiary or on the throne of England. . . . I must do something. I must be something.

—Nina King,
in a letter to her sister, Grace King

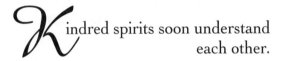

 $\mathcal{K}$ indred spirits soon understand
each other.

—*Eliza Leslie*

$\mathcal{F}$emale friendships are of rapid growth.

—*Benjamin Disraeli,*
Earl of Beaconsfield

*O*h! who the exquisite delights can tell,
The joy which mutual companionship imparts?

—*Mary Tighe*

*I*ntimacies between women often
go backwards, beginning in
revelations and ending in small talk
without loss of esteem.

—*Elizabeth Bowen*

*B*ut sparks electric only strike
On souls electrical alike

—*Hannah More*

We were a club, a society, a civilization all our own.

—*Annette, Cécile, Marie, and Yvonne Dionne (with James Brough)*

Some friendships are made by
nature, some by contact,
some by interest, and some by souls.

—*Jeremy Taylor*

*T*hick waters show no images of
things;
Friends are each other's mirrors, and
should be
Clearer than crystal, or the mountain
springs.

—*Katherine Fowler Philips*

$\mathcal{M}$y fellow, my companion, held
most dear,
My soul, my other self, my inward
friend

—*Mary Sidney Herbert*

*$\mathcal{B}$y building relations . . . we
create a source of love
and personal pride and belonging that
makes living in a chaotic world easier.*

—*Susan Lieberman*

$\mathcal{F}$or mem'ry painted this perfect day
  With colors that never fade,
And we find at the end of a perfect day
  The soul of a friend we've made.

—*Carrie Jacobs Bond*

 good friend is my
nearest relation.

—*Anonymous*

$\mathcal{N}$ear or far, there are burdens
and terrors in sisterhood.

—*Helen Yglesias*

am not afraid to trust my
sisters—not I.

—Angelina Grimké

There is something so physical about sisterhood; some body-memory, too deep for words.

—*Kennedy Fraser*

A true sister is a friend who
listens with her heart.

—*Anonymous*

I am thinking that I am being present at a spectacle which cynics say is impossible, the spectacle of a woman delighting—and with most obvious sincerity—in the beauty of another.

—*Dorothy Canfield Fisher*

$\mathcal{P}$erhaps there is nothing more lovely than the love of two beautiful women, who are not jealous of each other's charms.

—*Benjamin Disraeli, Earl of Beaconsfield*

$\mathcal{T}$he young ladies entered the
drawing-room in the full
fervor of sisterly animosity.

—R. S. Surtees

There is a space within sisterhood
for likeness and difference, for
the subtle differences that challenge and
delight; there is space for
disappointment—and surprise.

—*Christine Downing*

$\mathcal{A}$s nobody can do more mischief to a woman than a woman, so perhaps might one reverse the maxim and say nobody can do more good.

—*Elizabeth Holland*

*F*emale friendships that work are
   relationships in which women
help each other belong to themselves.

—*Louise Bernikow*

The sister bond is often greater
than with a friend or a
brother . . .

—*Harriette McAdoo*

I have seen in the mirror
and the eyes of my
sisters
that pretty is the
woman in darkness
who flowers with loving.

—*Chirlane McCray*

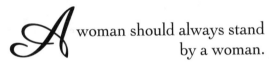

woman should always stand
by a woman.

— *Euripides*

We're just women who admire
and really know each other.
We allow each other to have the
weaknesses the public doesn't allow us
to have. . . .

—*Liza Minnelli,*
of her sister Lorna Luft

*R*elationships are a primary
source of self-esteem for
girls and women. . . .

—*Jeanne Elium and Don Elium*

$\mathcal{T}$he next generation of women
will enter a world in which
they are perceived to have more
opportunities for creating fulfilling lives
than women have ever had before.

—*Elizabeth Debold, Idelisse Malaye,
and Marie Wilson*

$\mathcal{V}$irtually all women today share a basic core of commitment to the family and to their own equality within and beyond it, as long as the family and the equality are not seen to be in conflict.

— Betty Friedan

*H*elp one another, is part of the
religion of our sisterhood.

—*Louisa May Alcott*

*B*eing a woman is a terribly difficult task, since it consists principally of dealing with men.

—Joseph Conrad

*W*omen are a sisterhood. They make common cause in behalf of the sex, and, indeed, this is natural enough, when we consider the vast power that the law gives us over them.

— *William Cobbett*

$\mathcal{W}$e are apt to be kinder to the brutes that love us than the women that love us. Is it because the brutes are dumb?

— George Eliot

*W*hatever women do they must
do it twice as well as men to
be thought half as good. Luckily, this is
not difficult.

—*Charlotte Whitton*

*A*ny woman who has a great
deal to offer the world is
in trouble.

—*Hazel Scott*

*M*en live by forgetting—women
live on memories.

—*T. S. Eliot*

$\mathcal{I}$t is only the women whose eyes have been washed clear with tears who get the broad vision that makes them little sisters to all the world.

—*Dorothy Dix*

$\mathcal{O}$ne gender to walk the wide
world in
Is the feminine,
A plight that — softly to a friend —
I can recommend.

—Helen Bevington

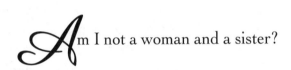

$\mathcal{A}$m I not a woman and a sister?

—*Anti-slavery motto*

𝒪f you sing too often of woe, yours or your sisters', you may be charged with being "too personal," "too autobiographical," too much a woman who cries out, who acknowledges openly, shamelessly, the pain of living and the joy of becoming free.

—*Nellie Wong*

*E*veryone needs reminders that the fact of their being on this earth is important and that each life changes everything.

—*Marge Kennedy*

'Tis the woman's strongest vindication for speaking that *the world needs to hear her voice*. . . . The world has had to limp along with the wobbling gait and one-sided hesitancy of a man with one eye. Suddenly the bandage is removed from the other eye and the whole body is filled with light. It sees a circle where before it saw a segment. The darkened eye restored, every member rejoices with it.

—Anna Julia Cooper

$\mathcal{S}$isterhood is powerful.

—*Robin Morgan*

Bibliography

Barbara Alpert. *No Friend Like a Sister: A Celebration in Words and Memories*. New York: Berkley Books, 1996.

Robert Andrews, ed. *The Cassell Dictionary of Contemporary Quotations*. London: Cassell Wellington House, 1996.

Robert Andrews, ed. *The Columbia Dictionary of Quotations*. New York: Columbia University Press, 1993.

Maturin M. Ballou, ed. *Notable Thoughts About Women*. Ann Arbor: Gryphon Books, 1971.

John Bartlett and Emily Morrison Beck, eds. *Bartlett's Familiar Quotations*. 15th. edition. Boston: Little, Brown, 1980.

J. M. and M. J. Cohen, eds. *The New Penguin Dictionary of Quotations*. New York: Penguin, 1996.

J. M. and M. J. Cohen, eds. *The Penguin Dictionary of Twentieth-Century Quotations*. London: Oxford University Press, 1993.

Lois Stiles Edgerly, ed. *Give Her This Day*. Maine: Tilbury House, 1990.

Eugene Ehrlic and Marshall De Bruh, eds. *The International Thesaurus of Quotations*. New York: Harper Collins, 1996.

Claudine Gandolfi, comp. *Sisters*. White Plains: Peter Pauper Press, 1997.

Susan Ginsberg, ed. *Family Wisdom*. New York: Columbia University Press, 1996.

Lois L. Kaufman, ed. *To My Daughter*. New York: Peter Pauper Press, 1990.

Philip Kelly and Ronald Hudson, eds. *The Brownings' Correspondence*. Kansas: Wedgestone Press, 1984.

Alec Lewis, ed. *The Quotable Quotations Book*. New York: Thomas Y. Crowell, 1980.

Illona Linthwaite, ed. *Ain't I a Woman*. New York: Wings Books, 1993.

Rosalie Maggio, ed. *The Beacon Book of Quotations by Women.* Boston: Beacon Press, 1992.

Rosalie Maggio, ed. *The New Beacon Book of Quotations by Women.* Boston: Beacon Press, 1996.

B. M. Orbach, ed. *A Token of Friendship.* New York: Clarkson N. Potter, 1987.

Elaine Partnow, ed. *The New Quotable Woman.* New York: Facts on File, 1992.

Elaine Partnow, ed. *The Quotable Woman: 1800–1981.* New York: Facts on File, 1982.

Elaine Partnow, ed. *The Quotable Woman: Eve–1799.* New York: Facts on File, 1985.

Laurence J. Peter, ed. *Peter's Quotations: Ideas for Our Time.* New York: William Morrow, 1977.

W. Safire and L. Safir, eds. *Words of Wisdom.* New York: Simon and Schuster, 1989.

Oscar Schoenfeld, ed. *Some Remembered Words.* Chicago: Academy Publishers, 1996.

James B. Simpson, ed. *Contemporary Quotations.* New York: Thomas Y. Crowell, 1964.

Burton Stevenson, ed. *The Home Book of Quotations Classical and Modern.* 9th. Edition. New York: Dodd, Mead, 1958.

Dorothy Uris, ed. *Say It Again.* New York: Dutton, 1979.

Carolyn Warner, ed. *The Last Word: A Treasury of Women's Quotes.* Englewood Cliffs: Prentice-Hall, 1992.

The Macmillan Dictionary of Quotations. New York: Macmillan, 1989.

Motherhood: A Gift of Love. Philadelphia: The Running Press, 1995.

The Oxford Dictionary of Quotations. 2nd. Edition. London: Oxford University Press, 1959.

My Sister: A Treasury of Companionship. Philadelphia: The Running Press, 1995.

My Sister, My Friend. Texas: Brownlow Publishing, 1993.